50 Classic American Pie Recipes

By: Kelly Johnson

Table of Contents

- Classic Apple Pie
- Southern Pecan Pie
- Traditional Pumpkin Pie
- Cherry Pie with Lattice Crust
- Blueberry Pie
- Key Lime Pie
- Banana Cream Pie
- Coconut Cream Pie
- Chocolate Silk Pie
- Lemon Meringue Pie
- Peanut Butter Pie
- Dutch Apple Pie (Crumb Topping)
- Bourbon Pecan Pie
- Sweet Potato Pie
- Blackberry Pie
- Raspberry Pie
- Strawberry Rhubarb Pie
- Chess Pie
- Shoofly Pie
- Boston Cream Pie
- Maple Walnut Pie
- Cranberry Apple Pie
- Chocolate Chip Cookie Pie
- Turtle Pie (Caramel, Chocolate, and Pecans)
- Butterscotch Pie
- Mississippi Mud Pie
- S'mores Pie
- Chocolate Peanut Butter Pie
- Honey Pie
- Molasses Pie
- Chess Pie with Cornmeal Crust
- Oatmeal Pie
- Rhubarb Custard Pie
- Pear and Ginger Pie
- Mango Pie

- Pineapple Cream Pie
- Grape Pie
- Vanilla Custard Pie
- Cream Cheese Pie
- Almond Joy Pie
- Elvis Pie (Banana, Peanut Butter, and Bacon)
- Brown Sugar Pie
- Mincemeat Pie
- Red Velvet Pie
- Peanut Butter and Jelly Pie
- Blackberry Peach Pie
- Eggnog Pie
- Pumpkin Cheesecake Pie
- Bourbon Chocolate Pie
- Caramel Apple Pie

Classic Apple Pie

Ingredients:

- 2 ½ cups all-purpose flour
- 1 teaspoon salt
- 1 cup unsalted butter, cold and cubed
- 6 tablespoons ice water
- 6 apples, peeled and sliced
- ¾ cup sugar
- 1 teaspoon cinnamon
- 1 tablespoon lemon juice
- 1 tablespoon cornstarch
- 1 egg (for egg wash)

Instructions:

1. Mix flour and salt, cut in butter, and add ice water to form dough. Chill for 1 hour.
2. Toss apples with sugar, cinnamon, lemon juice, and cornstarch.
3. Roll out dough, place in a pie dish, add filling, and cover with top crust.
4. Brush with egg wash and bake at 375°F (190°C) for 50 minutes.

Southern Pecan Pie

Ingredients:

- 1 unbaked pie crust
- 1 cup corn syrup
- ¾ cup brown sugar
- 3 eggs
- 1 teaspoon vanilla extract
- ¼ teaspoon salt
- 1 ½ cups pecans

Instructions:

1. Preheat oven to 350°F (175°C).
2. Whisk corn syrup, sugar, eggs, vanilla, and salt.
3. Stir in pecans and pour into crust.
4. Bake for 50–55 minutes until set.

Traditional Pumpkin Pie

Ingredients:

- 1 unbaked pie crust
- 1 can (15 oz) pumpkin puree
- ¾ cup brown sugar
- 1 teaspoon cinnamon
- ½ teaspoon nutmeg
- ½ teaspoon ginger
- ¼ teaspoon salt
- 3 eggs
- 1 cup evaporated milk

Instructions:

1. Preheat oven to 375°F (190°C).
2. Whisk pumpkin, sugar, spices, eggs, and milk.
3. Pour into crust and bake for 50–55 minutes.

Cherry Pie with Lattice Crust

Ingredients:

- 2 unbaked pie crusts
- 4 cups cherries, pitted
- ¾ cup sugar
- 1 tablespoon cornstarch
- 1 teaspoon lemon juice
- 1 teaspoon vanilla extract
- 1 egg (for egg wash)

Instructions:

1. Preheat oven to 375°F (190°C).
2. Mix cherries, sugar, cornstarch, lemon juice, and vanilla.
3. Pour into crust, create a lattice top with second crust, and brush with egg wash.
4. Bake for 45–50 minutes.

Blueberry Pie

Ingredients:

- 2 unbaked pie crusts
- 4 cups blueberries
- ¾ cup sugar
- 1 tablespoon lemon juice
- 2 tablespoons cornstarch
- 1 egg (for egg wash)

Instructions:

1. Preheat oven to 375°F (190°C).
2. Toss blueberries with sugar, lemon juice, and cornstarch.
3. Pour into crust, add top crust, and brush with egg wash.
4. Bake for 45–50 minutes.

Key Lime Pie

Ingredients:

- 1 graham cracker crust
- 1 can (14 oz) sweetened condensed milk
- ½ cup key lime juice
- 3 egg yolks
- Whipped cream for topping

Instructions:

1. Preheat oven to 350°F (175°C).
2. Whisk condensed milk, lime juice, and egg yolks.
3. Pour into crust and bake for 15 minutes.
4. Chill for 2 hours and top with whipped cream.

Banana Cream Pie

Ingredients:

- 1 pre-baked pie crust
- 3 bananas, sliced
- 2 cups milk
- ¾ cup sugar
- 3 egg yolks
- ¼ cup cornstarch
- 1 teaspoon vanilla extract
- Whipped cream for topping

Instructions:

1. Heat milk and sugar, then whisk in yolks and cornstarch until thick.
2. Stir in vanilla and pour over bananas in crust.
3. Chill for 2 hours, then top with whipped cream.

Coconut Cream Pie

Ingredients:

- 1 pre-baked pie crust
- 2 cups milk
- ¾ cup sugar
- ¼ cup cornstarch
- 3 egg yolks
- 1 teaspoon vanilla extract
- 1 cup shredded coconut
- Whipped cream for topping

Instructions:

1. Heat milk and sugar, then whisk in yolks and cornstarch until thick.
2. Stir in vanilla and coconut, then pour into crust.
3. Chill for 2 hours, then top with whipped cream.

Chocolate Silk Pie

Ingredients:

- 1 pre-baked pie crust
- 1 cup heavy cream
- ¾ cup dark chocolate, melted
- ½ cup butter, softened
- ¾ cup sugar
- 3 eggs
- 1 teaspoon vanilla extract

Instructions:

1. Melt chocolate and butter together.
2. Beat sugar and eggs until fluffy, then mix with chocolate.
3. Pour into crust and chill for 3 hours.
4. Top with whipped cream before serving.

Lemon Meringue Pie

Ingredients:

- **For the filling:**
    - 1 pre-baked pie crust
    - 1 cup sugar
    - ¼ cup cornstarch
    - 1 ½ cups water
    - 4 egg yolks
    - ½ cup lemon juice
    - 2 tablespoons butter
    - 1 teaspoon lemon zest
- **For the meringue:**
    - 4 egg whites
    - ¼ teaspoon cream of tartar
    - ½ cup sugar

Instructions:

1. Whisk sugar, cornstarch, and water in a saucepan over medium heat until thickened.
2. Slowly whisk in egg yolks, lemon juice, butter, and zest. Cook for 2 minutes.
3. Pour into the crust.
4. Beat egg whites and cream of tartar until soft peaks form. Gradually add sugar and beat until stiff peaks form.
5. Spread meringue over the filling and bake at 350°F (175°C) for 15 minutes until golden brown.

Peanut Butter Pie

Ingredients:

- 1 graham cracker crust
- 1 cup creamy peanut butter
- 8 oz cream cheese, softened
- 1 cup powdered sugar
- 1 cup whipped cream or Cool Whip

Instructions:

1. Beat peanut butter, cream cheese, and powdered sugar until smooth.
2. Fold in whipped cream and pour into the crust.
3. Chill for 2 hours before serving.

Dutch Apple Pie (Crumb Topping)

Ingredients:

- **For the filling:**
    - 1 unbaked pie crust
    - 6 apples, peeled and sliced
    - ¾ cup sugar
    - 1 teaspoon cinnamon
    - 1 tablespoon lemon juice
    - 1 tablespoon cornstarch
- **For the crumb topping:**
    - ¾ cup flour
    - ½ cup brown sugar
    - ½ teaspoon cinnamon
    - ½ cup butter, melted

Instructions:

1. Toss apples with sugar, cinnamon, lemon juice, and cornstarch.
2. Pour into crust.
3. Mix flour, brown sugar, cinnamon, and melted butter. Sprinkle over apples.
4. Bake at 375°F (190°C) for 45 minutes.

Bourbon Pecan Pie

Ingredients:

- 1 unbaked pie crust
- 1 cup pecans
- ¾ cup brown sugar
- 1 cup corn syrup
- 3 eggs
- 1 tablespoon bourbon
- 1 teaspoon vanilla extract
- ¼ teaspoon salt

Instructions:

1. Preheat oven to 350°F (175°C).
2. Whisk sugar, syrup, eggs, bourbon, vanilla, and salt.
3. Stir in pecans and pour into crust.
4. Bake for 50–55 minutes until set.

Sweet Potato Pie

Ingredients:

- 1 unbaked pie crust
- 2 cups mashed sweet potatoes
- ¾ cup sugar
- ½ cup evaporated milk
- 2 eggs
- 1 teaspoon cinnamon
- ½ teaspoon nutmeg
- 1 teaspoon vanilla extract

Instructions:

1. Preheat oven to 375°F (190°C).
2. Whisk all ingredients together until smooth.
3. Pour into crust and bake for 50–55 minutes.

Blackberry Pie

Ingredients:

- 2 unbaked pie crusts
- 4 cups blackberries
- ¾ cup sugar
- 1 tablespoon lemon juice
- 2 tablespoons cornstarch
- 1 egg (for egg wash)

Instructions:

1. Preheat oven to 375°F (190°C).
2. Toss blackberries with sugar, lemon juice, and cornstarch.
3. Pour into crust, add top crust, and brush with egg wash.
4. Bake for 45–50 minutes.

Raspberry Pie

Ingredients:

- 2 unbaked pie crusts
- 4 cups raspberries
- ¾ cup sugar
- 2 tablespoons cornstarch
- 1 tablespoon lemon juice
- 1 egg (for egg wash)

Instructions:

1. Preheat oven to 375°F (190°C).
2. Toss raspberries with sugar, cornstarch, and lemon juice.
3. Pour into crust, add top crust, and brush with egg wash.
4. Bake for 45 minutes.

Strawberry Rhubarb Pie

Ingredients:

- 2 unbaked pie crusts
- 3 cups sliced strawberries
- 2 cups chopped rhubarb
- ¾ cup sugar
- 2 tablespoons cornstarch
- 1 teaspoon vanilla extract
- 1 egg (for egg wash)

Instructions:

1. Preheat oven to 375°F (190°C).
2. Toss strawberries and rhubarb with sugar, cornstarch, and vanilla.
3. Pour into crust, add top crust, and brush with egg wash.
4. Bake for 45–50 minutes.

Chess Pie

Ingredients:

- 1 unbaked pie crust
- 1 ½ cups sugar
- ½ cup butter, melted
- 4 eggs
- 1 tablespoon cornmeal
- 1 teaspoon vanilla extract
- ¼ cup milk

Instructions:

1. Preheat oven to 350°F (175°C).
2. Whisk sugar, butter, eggs, cornmeal, vanilla, and milk.
3. Pour into crust and bake for 50 minutes.

Shoofly Pie

Ingredients:

- 1 unbaked pie crust
- 1 cup molasses
- ¾ cup hot water
- ½ teaspoon baking soda
- 1 egg, beaten
- 1 cup flour
- ½ cup brown sugar
- ¼ cup butter, melted

Instructions:

1. Preheat oven to 375°F (190°C).
2. Mix molasses, water, baking soda, and egg. Pour into crust.
3. Combine flour, brown sugar, and butter to make crumbs. Sprinkle over filling.
4. Bake for 45 minutes.

Boston Cream Pie

Ingredients:

- **For the cake:**
    - 1 ½ cups flour
    - 1 teaspoon baking powder
    - ½ teaspoon salt
    - ½ cup butter, softened
    - ¾ cup sugar
    - 2 eggs
    - 1 teaspoon vanilla extract
    - ½ cup milk
- **For the filling:**
    - 1 cup milk
    - ¼ cup sugar
    - 1 egg yolk
    - 1 tablespoon cornstarch
    - 1 teaspoon vanilla extract
- **For the chocolate glaze:**
    - ½ cup heavy cream
    - ½ cup dark chocolate chips

Instructions:

1. Bake the cake layers at 350°F (175°C) for 25 minutes.
2. Cook milk, sugar, egg yolk, cornstarch, and vanilla for the filling until thick.
3. Layer filling between cakes.
4. Heat cream and stir in chocolate until smooth, then pour over cake.

Maple Walnut Pie

Ingredients:

- 1 unbaked pie crust
- ¾ cup maple syrup
- ½ cup brown sugar
- 3 eggs
- 1 teaspoon vanilla extract
- ¼ teaspoon salt
- 1 cup chopped walnuts

Instructions:

1. Preheat oven to 350°F (175°C).
2. Whisk syrup, sugar, eggs, vanilla, and salt.
3. Stir in walnuts and pour into crust.
4. Bake for 50 minutes.

Cranberry Apple Pie

Ingredients:

- 2 unbaked pie crusts
- 3 cups apples, sliced
- 1 cup cranberries
- ¾ cup sugar
- 1 tablespoon lemon juice
- 1 teaspoon cinnamon
- 2 tablespoons cornstarch
- 1 egg (for egg wash)

Instructions:

1. Toss apples and cranberries with sugar, lemon juice, cinnamon, and cornstarch.
2. Pour into crust, add top crust, and brush with egg wash.
3. Bake at 375°F (190°C) for 50 minutes.

Chocolate Chip Cookie Pie

Ingredients:

- 1 unbaked pie crust
- 1 cup brown sugar
- ½ cup butter, melted
- 2 eggs
- 1 teaspoon vanilla extract
- ½ cup flour
- ½ teaspoon salt
- 1 cup chocolate chips

Instructions:

1. Preheat oven to 350°F (175°C).
2. Mix sugar, butter, eggs, vanilla, flour, and salt.
3. Stir in chocolate chips and pour into crust.
4. Bake for 45 minutes.

Turtle Pie (Caramel, Chocolate, and Pecans)

Ingredients:

- 1 graham cracker crust
- 1 cup caramel sauce
- 1 cup chopped pecans
- 1 cup chocolate chips, melted
- 1 cup whipped cream

Instructions:

1. Pour caramel sauce into crust and sprinkle with pecans.
2. Drizzle with melted chocolate.
3. Top with whipped cream and chill for 2 hours.

Butterscotch Pie

Ingredients:

- 1 pre-baked pie crust
- 1 cup brown sugar
- ¼ cup butter
- 2 cups milk
- 3 egg yolks
- ¼ cup cornstarch
- 1 teaspoon vanilla extract

Instructions:

1. Cook sugar and butter until melted.
2. Whisk in milk, yolks, and cornstarch, cooking until thick.
3. Stir in vanilla and pour into crust.
4. Chill for 2 hours before serving.

Mississippi Mud Pie

Ingredients:

- 1 chocolate cookie crust
- 1 cup chocolate chips, melted
- 1 cup sugar
- ½ cup butter, melted
- 3 eggs
- 1 teaspoon vanilla extract
- ½ cup heavy cream

Instructions:

1. Preheat oven to 350°F (175°C).
2. Whisk chocolate, sugar, butter, eggs, vanilla, and cream.
3. Pour into crust and bake for 40 minutes.

S'mores Pie

Ingredients:

- 1 graham cracker crust
- 1 cup chocolate chips, melted
- 1 cup mini marshmallows
- ½ cup heavy cream

Instructions:

1. Melt chocolate and mix with heavy cream. Pour into crust.
2. Top with marshmallows and broil for 1–2 minutes until golden.

Chocolate Peanut Butter Pie

Ingredients:

- 1 chocolate cookie crust
- 1 cup peanut butter
- 8 oz cream cheese, softened
- 1 cup powdered sugar
- 1 cup whipped cream

Instructions:

1. Mix peanut butter, cream cheese, and sugar until smooth.
2. Fold in whipped cream and pour into crust.
3. Chill for 2 hours.

Honey Pie

Ingredients:

- 1 pre-baked pie crust
- ¾ cup honey
- ½ cup heavy cream
- 3 eggs
- ½ teaspoon cinnamon

Instructions:

1. Whisk honey, cream, eggs, and cinnamon.
2. Pour into crust and bake at 350°F (175°C) for 40 minutes.

Molasses Pie

Ingredients:

- 1 unbaked pie crust
- 1 cup molasses
- ¾ cup brown sugar
- ¼ cup butter, melted
- 3 eggs
- 1 teaspoon vanilla extract

Instructions:

1. Preheat oven to 350°F (175°C).
2. Mix molasses, sugar, butter, eggs, and vanilla.
3. Pour into crust and bake for 45 minutes.

Chess Pie with Cornmeal Crust

Ingredients:

- **For the crust:**
    - 1 ½ cups flour
    - ¼ cup cornmeal
    - ½ teaspoon salt
    - ½ cup cold butter, cubed
    - 3 tablespoons ice water
- **For the filling:**
    - 1 ½ cups sugar
    - ½ cup butter, melted
    - 4 eggs
    - ¼ cup buttermilk
    - 1 teaspoon vanilla extract
    - 1 tablespoon cornmeal

Instructions:

1. Mix flour, cornmeal, and salt. Cut in butter, add ice water, and form dough. Chill for 30 minutes.
2. Roll out dough, place in a pie dish, and pre-bake at 375°F (190°C) for 10 minutes.
3. Whisk sugar, butter, eggs, buttermilk, vanilla, and cornmeal. Pour into crust.
4. Bake at 350°F (175°C) for 45–50 minutes.

Oatmeal Pie

Ingredients:

- 1 unbaked pie crust
- 1 cup rolled oats
- ¾ cup brown sugar
- ½ cup corn syrup
- 3 eggs
- ½ cup butter, melted
- 1 teaspoon vanilla extract

Instructions:

1. Preheat oven to 350°F (175°C).
2. Mix oats, sugar, corn syrup, eggs, butter, and vanilla.
3. Pour into crust and bake for 50 minutes.

Rhubarb Custard Pie

Ingredients:

- 1 unbaked pie crust
- 3 cups rhubarb, chopped
- ¾ cup sugar
- 2 eggs
- 1 cup heavy cream
- 1 tablespoon flour
- 1 teaspoon vanilla extract

Instructions:

1. Preheat oven to 375°F (190°C).
2. Toss rhubarb with sugar and flour.
3. Whisk eggs, cream, and vanilla. Pour over rhubarb in crust.
4. Bake for 45 minutes.

Pear and Ginger Pie

Ingredients:

- 2 unbaked pie crusts
- 4 pears, peeled and sliced
- ¾ cup sugar
- 1 tablespoon grated fresh ginger
- 1 tablespoon cornstarch
- 1 teaspoon lemon juice
- 1 egg (for egg wash)

Instructions:

1. Toss pears with sugar, ginger, cornstarch, and lemon juice.
2. Pour into crust, add top crust, and brush with egg wash.
3. Bake at 375°F (190°C) for 50 minutes.

Mango Pie

Ingredients:

- 1 unbaked pie crust
- 3 cups mango, diced
- ¾ cup sugar
- 1 tablespoon cornstarch
- 1 teaspoon lime juice
- ½ teaspoon cinnamon

Instructions:

1. Toss mango with sugar, cornstarch, lime juice, and cinnamon.
2. Pour into crust and bake at 375°F (190°C) for 45 minutes.

Pineapple Cream Pie

Ingredients:

- 1 pre-baked pie crust
- 1 can (20 oz) crushed pineapple, drained
- ½ cup sugar
- 2 cups milk
- 3 egg yolks
- ¼ cup cornstarch
- 1 teaspoon vanilla extract
- Whipped cream for topping

Instructions:

1. Heat milk, sugar, egg yolks, cornstarch, and vanilla over medium heat until thick.
2. Stir in pineapple and pour into crust.
3. Chill for 2 hours and top with whipped cream.

Grape Pie

Ingredients:

- 2 unbaked pie crusts
- 4 cups Concord grapes, peeled and seeded
- ¾ cup sugar
- 1 tablespoon lemon juice
- 1 tablespoon cornstarch
- 1 egg (for egg wash)

Instructions:

1. Cook grapes, sugar, lemon juice, and cornstarch until thickened.
2. Pour into crust, add top crust, and brush with egg wash.
3. Bake at 375°F (190°C) for 50 minutes.

Vanilla Custard Pie

Ingredients:

- 1 pre-baked pie crust
- 2 cups milk
- ¾ cup sugar
- 3 eggs
- ¼ cup cornstarch
- 1 teaspoon vanilla extract
- ½ teaspoon nutmeg

Instructions:

1. Heat milk and sugar, then whisk in eggs, cornstarch, and vanilla.
2. Pour into crust and bake at 350°F (175°C) for 40 minutes.
3. Sprinkle with nutmeg before serving.

Cream Cheese Pie

Ingredients:

- 1 graham cracker crust
- 8 oz cream cheese, softened
- ½ cup sugar
- 1 teaspoon vanilla extract
- 1 cup whipped cream

Instructions:

1. Beat cream cheese, sugar, and vanilla until smooth.
2. Fold in whipped cream and pour into crust.
3. Chill for 2 hours before serving.

Almond Joy Pie

Ingredients:

- 1 chocolate cookie crust
- 1 cup shredded coconut
- ½ cup sliced almonds
- 1 cup chocolate chips, melted
- 1 cup heavy cream

Instructions:

1. Mix coconut, almonds, melted chocolate, and cream.
2. Pour into crust and chill for 2 hours.

Elvis Pie (Banana, Peanut Butter, and Bacon)

Ingredients:

- 1 graham cracker crust
- 2 bananas, sliced
- ½ cup peanut butter
- 8 oz cream cheese, softened
- ½ cup sugar
- 1 cup whipped cream
- 4 slices cooked bacon, crumbled

Instructions:

1. Beat peanut butter, cream cheese, and sugar until smooth.
2. Fold in whipped cream and stir in bacon.
3. Layer bananas in crust, pour filling over, and chill for 2 hours.

Brown Sugar Pie

Ingredients:

- 1 unbaked pie crust
- 1 ½ cups brown sugar
- ½ cup butter, melted
- 3 eggs
- ¼ cup heavy cream
- 1 teaspoon vanilla extract
- ¼ teaspoon salt

Instructions:

1. Preheat oven to 350°F (175°C).
2. Whisk brown sugar, butter, eggs, cream, vanilla, and salt until smooth.
3. Pour into crust and bake for 45 minutes until set.

Mincemeat Pie

Ingredients:

- 2 unbaked pie crusts
- 2 cups mincemeat filling
- 1 tablespoon brandy or rum (optional)
- 1 egg (for egg wash)

Instructions:

1. Preheat oven to 375°F (190°C).
2. Stir brandy into mincemeat and pour into crust.
3. Add top crust, brush with egg wash, and bake for 40–45 minutes.

Red Velvet Pie

Ingredients:

- 1 chocolate cookie crust
- 8 oz cream cheese, softened
- ¾ cup sugar
- ½ cup buttermilk
- 2 eggs
- 1 teaspoon cocoa powder
- 1 teaspoon vanilla extract
- 1 teaspoon red food coloring

Instructions:

1. Preheat oven to 350°F (175°C).
2. Beat cream cheese, sugar, buttermilk, eggs, cocoa, vanilla, and red food coloring.
3. Pour into crust and bake for 40 minutes.

Peanut Butter and Jelly Pie

Ingredients:

- 1 graham cracker crust
- ¾ cup peanut butter
- 8 oz cream cheese, softened
- ½ cup powdered sugar
- 1 cup whipped cream
- ½ cup strawberry or grape jelly

Instructions:

1. Beat peanut butter, cream cheese, and powdered sugar until smooth.
2. Fold in whipped cream and spread into crust.
3. Swirl jelly on top and chill for 2 hours.

Blackberry Peach Pie

Ingredients:

- 2 unbaked pie crusts
- 2 cups blackberries
- 2 cups peaches, sliced
- ¾ cup sugar
- 2 tablespoons cornstarch
- 1 tablespoon lemon juice
- 1 egg (for egg wash)

Instructions:

1. Toss blackberries and peaches with sugar, cornstarch, and lemon juice.
2. Pour into crust, add top crust, and brush with egg wash.
3. Bake at 375°F (190°C) for 50 minutes.

Eggnog Pie

Ingredients:

- 1 graham cracker crust
- 1 cup eggnog
- ½ cup sugar
- 2 eggs
- ¼ cup cornstarch
- 1 teaspoon vanilla extract
- ½ teaspoon nutmeg

Instructions:

1. Heat eggnog, sugar, eggs, cornstarch, and vanilla over medium heat until thick.
2. Pour into crust and chill for 2 hours.
3. Sprinkle with nutmeg before serving.

Pumpkin Cheesecake Pie

Ingredients:

- 1 graham cracker crust
- 8 oz cream cheese, softened
- ½ cup sugar
- 1 cup pumpkin puree
- 1 teaspoon cinnamon
- ½ teaspoon nutmeg
- 2 eggs
- 1 teaspoon vanilla extract

Instructions:

1. Preheat oven to 350°F (175°C).
2. Beat cream cheese, sugar, pumpkin, spices, eggs, and vanilla.
3. Pour into crust and bake for 50 minutes.

Bourbon Chocolate Pie

Ingredients:

- 1 unbaked pie crust
- 1 cup dark chocolate chips, melted
- ½ cup butter, melted
- ¾ cup sugar
- 3 eggs
- ¼ cup bourbon
- 1 teaspoon vanilla extract

Instructions:

1. Preheat oven to 350°F (175°C).
2. Whisk chocolate, butter, sugar, eggs, bourbon, and vanilla.
3. Pour into crust and bake for 45 minutes.

Caramel Apple Pie

Ingredients:

- 2 unbaked pie crusts
- 6 apples, peeled and sliced
- ¾ cup caramel sauce
- ¾ cup sugar
- 1 teaspoon cinnamon
- 2 tablespoons cornstarch
- 1 tablespoon lemon juice
- 1 egg (for egg wash)

Instructions:

1. Toss apples with caramel, sugar, cinnamon, cornstarch, and lemon juice.
2. Pour into crust, add top crust, and brush with egg wash.
3. Bake at 375°F (190°C) for 50 minutes.

www.ingramcontent.com/pod-product-compliance
Lightning Source LLC
LaVergne TN
LVHW081333060526
838201LV00055B/2619